A Question of Geography

What makes a mega city mega?

and other questions about SETTLEMENTS

Paula and Tony Richardson

WAYLAND

First published in Great Britain in 2024
by Wayland

© Hodder and Stoughton, 2024

Credits:
Editors: Julia Bird; Julia Adams
Design and illustrations: Matt Lilly
Cover design: Matt Lilly

HB ISBN 978 1 5263 2662 1
PB ISBN 978 1 5263 2663 8

Printed and bound in Dubai

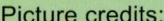

MIX
Paper | Supporting
responsible forestry
FSC® C104740
FSC
www.fsc.org

Picture credits:

Alamy: Lakeview Images 21; Iain Masterton 26-27c;
Frederic Reglain 24.
Shutterstock: Aanimesh 8c; Acsen 5t; Jawwad Ali 11b;
Bildagentur Zoonar GmbH 23b; Cortyn 11t; Cpyusef 29t;
F11 photo 16; Fritz16 23tl; Herb Klein 14tr;
Mr Wijannarongk Kunchit 26c; Marco Taliani de Marchio 19t;
Mistervlad 9b; Mark Oleksiy 20; Polar media 22b; Sakaret 28;
Shutterupiere 17t; Taiga f cover 6-7b; Tongarirokid 25; Travelview 15t;
Vladsilver 4t; Wasiolka 12b; WitR 18c; Youli Zhao 23b.

Every effort has been made to clear copyright.
Should there be any inadvertent omission,
please apply to the publisher for rectification

Wayland
An imprint of
Hachette Children's Group
Part of Hodder and Stoughton
Carmelite House
50 Victoria Embankment
London EC4Y 0DZ

An Hachette UK Company
www.hachette.co.uk
www.hachettechildrens.co.uk

Contents

What are settlements?

Settlements are places where people live together. They can be found in virtually every part of the world – only icy, remote Antarctica has no permanent settlements.

WE'RE PRETTY SETTLED HERE!

But how did settlements grow and take shape?

HOPE WE'RE NOT SHARING WITH A BEAR!

Hunting and gathering

Early humans didn't live in one place all year round. Instead, they moved around with the seasons, hunting, fishing and gathering local fruits, vegetables and seeds for food. They slept in natural shelters, such as caves or under cliffs. This lifestyle is known as nomadic and people still follow it in some places today (see pages 26–27).

Settling down

Around 12,000 years ago, a huge change happened in human civilisation. It is believed to have begun in an area of the Middle East that we now call the 'Fertile Crescent'. People began planting simple crops, such as cereals, to eat, and keeping animals for their meat, eggs and milk. People built permanent homes where they were farming. Over time, settlements grew.

The remains of the first known settlement, Çatalhöyük, in today's Turkey. It had no streets; instead, people walked across house roofs, and entered buildings from there, too.

HOME SWEET PREHISTORIC HOME!

What attracted people to live somewhere?

For early people, the natural landscape helped them decide where to settle. Fertile farming land was very important and it was good to be close to a source of water, such as a river, for drinking, washing and irrigating crops. Being near water also helped people to travel around by boat and to trade with nearby settlements, while building on higher land made places easier to defend.

Today we live in settlements all over the world. But how did they grow and why are they all so different? The best way to find out is by asking questions, so ask away!

What makes a mega city

Settlements can be tiny hamlets with just a few inhabitants, or huge cities, with populations of millions!

These are known as mega cities.

① Hamlet home
A hamlet is a small group of rural houses, without any local shops or services.

④ City living
Cities are big urban centres, with populations of 100,000 people or more. Many people live in or travel to cities for work, higher education, healthcare and entertainment.

⑤ Make it mega!
Mega cities have populations of over 10 million people. These huge, sprawling settlements are centres of work and learning, with a wealth of services, such as hospitals, sports facilities, theatres and museums, and shops. They also have good transport systems. Many mega cities are capital cities, where the country's government is based. Famous mega cities include Tokyo, New York and Delhi.

mega?

★

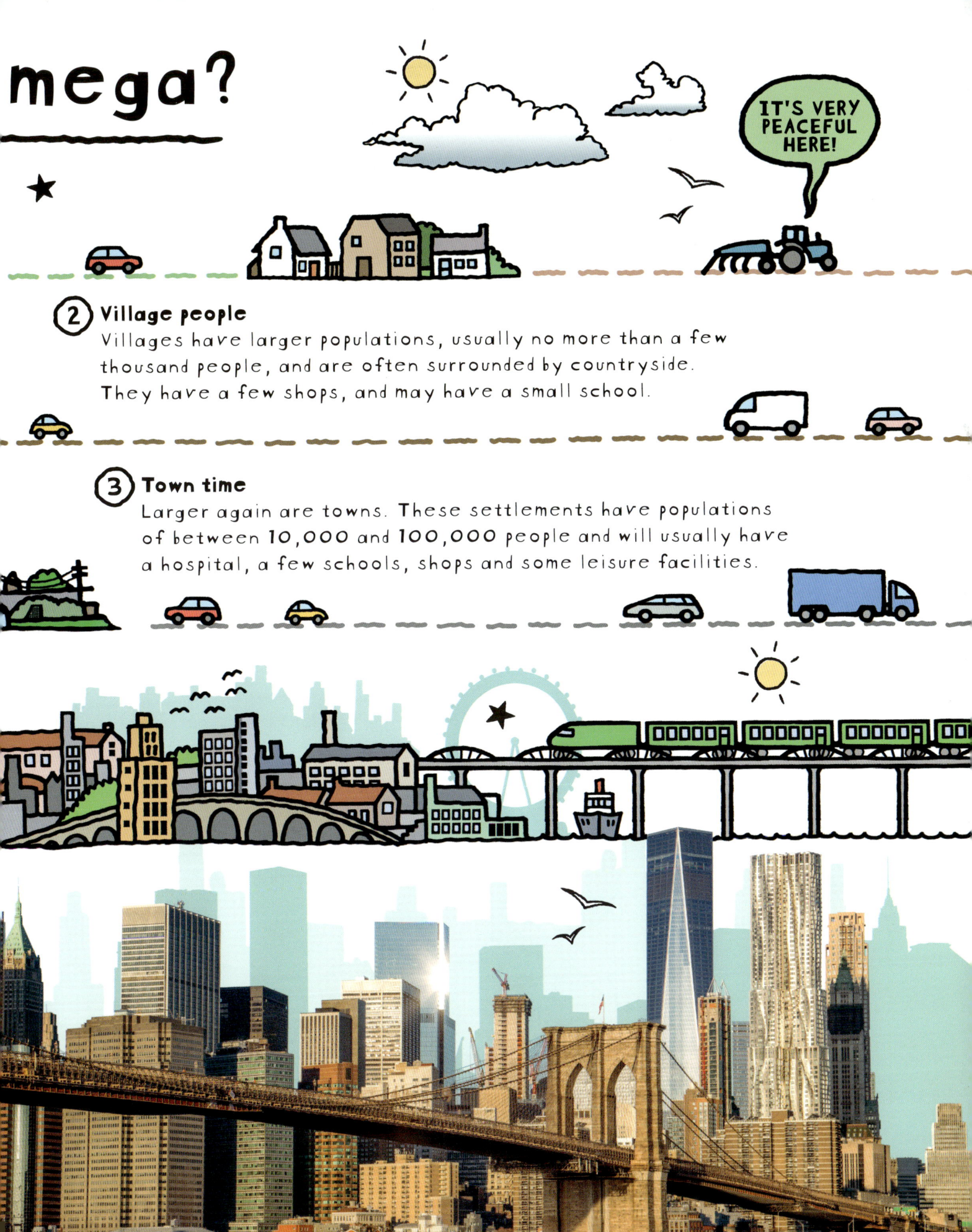

IT'S VERY PEACEFUL HERE!

② Village people

Villages have larger populations, usually no more than a few thousand people, and are often surrounded by countryside. They have a few shops, and may have a small school.

③ Town time

Larger again are towns. These settlements have populations of between 10,000 and 100,000 people and will usually have a hospital, a few schools, shops and some leisure facilities.

Do people sleep in dormitory towns?

Well – yes! Some settlements, such as dormitory towns, develop for a particular reason, including their location, purpose or the resources they have nearby.

Many of the world's largest cities, such as Mumbai, India, are close to the sea.

By the water

Settlements often grow up around sources of water, such as bigger rivers or sea harbours. Here, people can transport and trade their goods by boat or ship, creating lots of jobs and often making the settlement wealthy.

To market!

Many towns and cities have developed around marketplaces, where people such as farmers and craftspeople have gathered to buy and sell goods since ancient times.

I'LL SWAP YOU THESE TURNIPS FOR THAT POT!

DEAL! OH WAIT, I WON'T HAVE ANYTHING TO COOK THEM IN!

Big business

Industrial towns may grow up close to a source of raw materials, for example coal or iron mines. The materials are extracted and processed in the town's factories, creating jobs and attracting people to the town.

Seaside fun

Settlements often develop around the coast. Here, people come to enjoy time by the sea or may retire when they have finished working.

Centres of power

Cities where a country's government offices are based are usually big and influential. They are often the country's most important city.

The Reichstag building in Germany's capital, Berlin, is the seat of the country's parliament.

Sleepy towns

Dormitory towns grow up close to big cities, offering people more affordable or bigger places to live. People travel – or commute – to work in the city during the day and return to the dormitory town in the evening.

Wait – I live in a Roman city?

You might! Most cities around the world grew up over time and have an interesting (and sometimes very ancient) history.

Battlers and builders

The Roman Empire lasted for over 1,000 years. The Romans were brilliant engineers and the towns and cities they built across their empire had a structure that is still recognisable today.

ARE WE PLANNING OR PLAYING?

BOTH!

The Roman way

Roman settlements were usually based on a grid plan. Streets criss-crossed each other in a regular pattern, like a gigantic version of noughts and crosses. This made finding your way around nice and easy! At the centre of the town was a square, or forum, with important buildings and a marketplace.

Timgad was built in 100 BCE. Its ruins, including the towering Arch of Trajan, are very well preserved.

Great grids

Today, there are still towns and cities that have streets originally laid out during Roman times. You can see this grid pattern in the ruins of the ancient city of Timgad in Algeria, for example.

Planned cities in the USA like Chicago, San Francisco and New York were also based on a grid lay-out. This plan is still often followed when building new towns and cities around the world.

Odour-free cities!

The Romans weren't the only great — or even the first — builders of the ancient world. From around 2500 BCE the people of the Indus River Valley Civilisation, in today's Pakistan, built the great cities of Harappa and Mohenjo-daro. They had a grid-based lay-out of streets and houses, water supply and even toilet facilities.

Mohenjo-daro's citizens had access to over 700 wells for drinking water.

How are some towns like magnets?

Well, not real magnets obviously. But some places do attract lots of people to live in them, thanks to a variety of different reasons.

Feel the pull ...

Things that make people want to live in or move to a place are known as **PULL** factors. One of the biggest pull factors is work. People move to places where there are more jobs available, so they can earn money. Good housing and public services are another big pull factor.

People want to settle in places where they and their children can get a good education, use facilities such as parks or swimming pools and receive better healthcare.

The population of Sydney, Australia, is growing by tens of thousands each year.

The good life

A better quality of life also draws people to live in certain places. Many people like to live where the weather is neither too hot nor too cold and where the surroundings are clean and nice to look at.

Many people like to live near the sea.

Pushed out

The opposite to pull factors are **PUSH** factors. These are reasons that make people want to leave a place. They can include a lack of jobs and housing, poor public services, high crime rates or even war, and living in places at risk of natural disasters such as floods, earthquakes or volcanic eruptions.

City living

Cities and towns have a strong pull. In 1950 around a third of the world's population lived in urban areas. Today, more than half does, and that's expected to grow to two thirds of the world's population by 2050.

☐ RURAL POPULATION   ☐ URBAN POPULATION

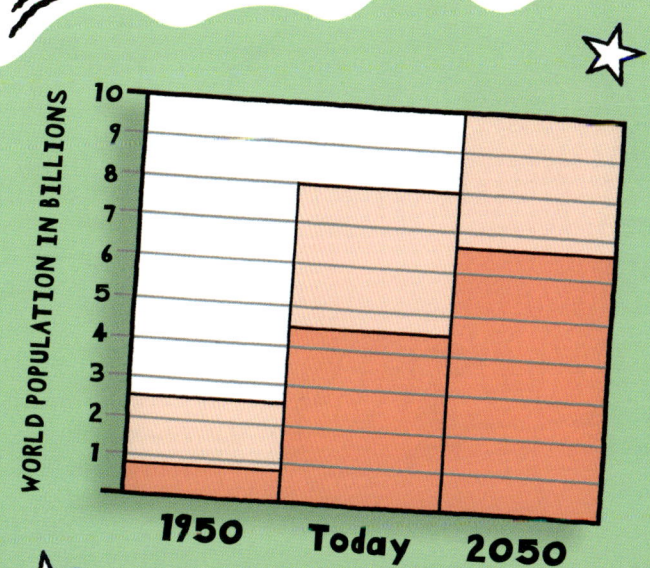

Was a city really named after cows?

QUEEN VICTORIA VILLE!

Sort of! Place names can have a fascinating history that tells us a lot about why and how the settlements came to be.

Famous figures

Many places are named after the people who founded the settlement, or for famous historical figures. According to legend, Rome, the capital city of Italy, was founded by the twins Romulus and Remus. Romulus killed Remus in a fight, and so Rome was named after him!

Settlements all over the world bear the name of Queen Victoria, who ruled the huge British Empire in the 19th century.

Hills and rivers

Places are often named after an important local feature, such as a hill, river or port. For example, the port city of Hong Kong is *Heung Gong* in Cantonese, which means 'Fragrant Harbour'!

Places can also be named for the reason that the settlement grew up there. Oxford, in the UK, was originally known as 'Oxanforda', meaning a place to ford, or cross, a river with your ox. Good to know!

OXANFORDA CROSS HERE!

Names from far away

When Europeans settled new lands, they often took place names with them. Former European colonies such as the US, Canada and Australia, have cities with names that combine 'New' with the name of an original settlement. For example, New York is named for York in the UK, and New Orleans for the French city of Orléans.

First names

Today, many places are reclaiming the names given to them by their Indigenous inhabitants. In Australia, for example, cities are now known by both the Indigenous name of the area, and by the name later given by European settlers.

Garramilla (Darwin)

Boorloo (Perth)

AUSTRALIA

Meanjin (Brisbane)

Warrane (Sydney)

Tarntanya (Adelaide)

Ngambri (Canberra)

Naarm (Melbourne)

nipaluna (Hobart)

How did polar bears save a town?

Settlements are changing all the time in different ways;

some grOW, while others shrink.

This is often thanks to push and pull factors (see pages 12–13), but settlements can change for surprising and unexpected reasons too!

Getting bigger ...

Tokyo, capital of Japan, began life as a quiet fishing village known as Edo, meaning 'estuary'. It grew from the 12th century, when the Edo clan built a castle there. In 1889, it was named Tokyo, meaning 'Eastern capital'.

Today, Tokyo is the centre of Japan's economy and government and the most populous city in the world, with a population of 37.4 million.

The huge population has led to a shortage of housing and grid-locked traffic. The government has started offering people money to move away from the capital.

WHAT HAPPENED TO EDO?!

WHERE'S EVERYBODY GONE?

Getting smaller ...

Other settlements have shrunk or even been abandoned over time. This is often caused by jobs disappearing. Across California, USA, a 'gold rush' in the 19th century led to towns springing up to house the gold hunters. But when the gold disappeared, so did the people, and the towns were abandoned. Sometimes, a natural disaster can damage a settlement so completely that living there is no longer possible (more on this on pages 18–19).

Polar watch!

Sometimes a settlement has to change to survive. The Canadian town of Churchill was once part of the fur trade. Now it has moved from hunting animals to watching them! Tourists visit to see polar bears, beluga whales, Arctic foxes, moose and wolves.

SAY CHEESE!

Can some places just ... disappear?

Believe it or not, yes, some settlements can just vanish. This can be because of a sudden natural disaster – or more man-made reasons.

VILLAGE CANNOT BE FOUND

Violent volcano

Pompeii was a thriving Roman city when the volcano Vesuvius erupted in 79 CE and destroyed it, along with the nearby town of Herculaneum. Many people escaped, but thousands died when massive hot clouds of ash and gas smothered the settlements.

Drowned town

Back in the 17th century, Port Royal in Jamaica was known as **'THE WICKEDEST CITY ON EARTH'**, as it was home to pirates. But in June 1692, an earthquake and then a tsunami struck the town, making it sink beneath the water. Port Royal is today a small fishing village, but the ruins of the once famous pirate port have been preserved under the sea.

ARRRGH! WHERE DID THE PORT GO?

Moved by man

Sometimes, settlements can vanish for a more practical purpose. Villages and hamlets have been deliberately flooded to create reservoirs, and their inhabitants rehomed nearby. Today, small settlements are still demolished to make room for new roads or to access natural resources, such as coal.

HELP!

Sometimes, flooded settlements start reappearing when the water levels are low, such as here, in Lake Resia, Italy.

Drowning homes

Rising sea levels, due to climate change, are putting coastal settlements at risk. People living in Pantai Bahagia, a village in Indonesia, have been forced to move as every high tide brings the sea into their homes. In a few years, the village may be totally under water.

GRRR, HIGH TIDE AGAIN.

What drove city commuters underground?

Well, wherever people live, they need to be able to get around! Public transport in towns and cities is always changing to keep up with our lives.

SORRY!

Mind the poo!

Cities in Europe and the USA got a **LOT** bigger during the Industrial Revolution (c.1760–1840), when huge numbers of people moved to the city to work in new factories.

Before this, most people travelled around on foot or by horse-drawn coach. In the 1830s, the first omnibuses took to the streets of London and Paris. These horse-drawn vehicles could carry up to 20 people to work and home again. They were slow though, and their poo made the streets pretty smelly!

Let the train take the strain

Workers got a new way to commute when the first train lines appeared in cities in the 19th century. People were able to move further away from their workplaces, and the first suburbs appeared around the edges of cities. Living further out meant a bigger house and cleaner surroundings, but not everyone could afford the cost of commuting.

Going underground ...

An exciting new solution to moving people around cities was the first underground railway, introduced in London in 1863.

Deep below the busy city streets, journeys became much faster. Paris, Budapest and New York introduced underground railways soon after, and they are now found all over the world, carrying millions of people every day.

Aldgate underground station, London, 1878.

The Clean Green Tram Machine

Electric trams were first used in Berlin, Germany in 1881 and other cities around the world soon followed their lead.

But by the 20th century, cars were much more widely owned and lots of tram routes disappeared. Today, though, trams are making a comeback! They offer commuters a quick, non-polluting journey to work. Melbourne in Australia has the largest tram network in the world, covering 250 km.

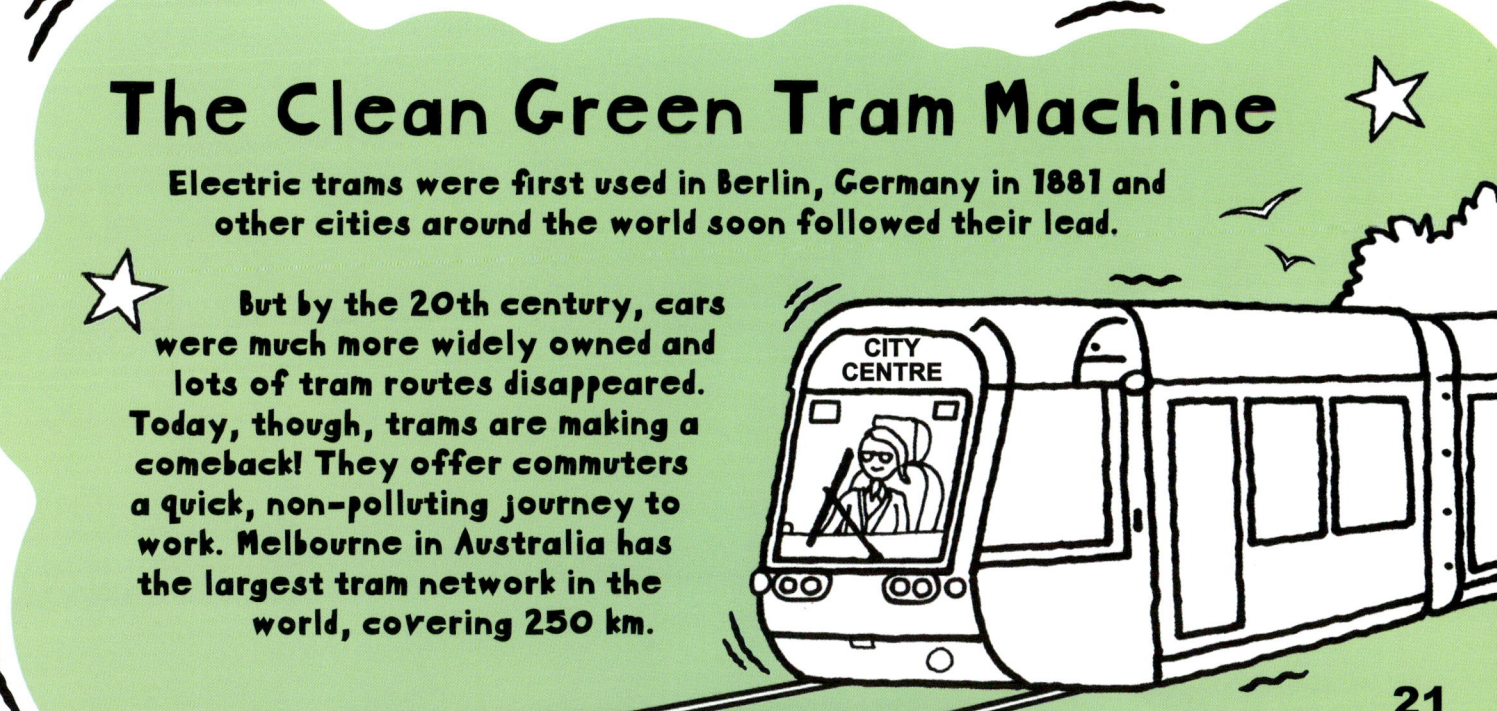

Is there really a town that lives in one building?

GREAT VIEWS!

Not quite, but almost! Around the world, people have adapted to live in some very extreme settlements.

Top of the world

Nuuk in Greenland is the world's most northerly capital, so – unsurprisingly – average daily temperatures are below freezing for half of the year. **BRRR**. The tiny city is even cut off from the rest of Greenland as there are no roads in and out of the city. But there are some positives to life in chilly Nuuk – it has its own (small) university and is one of the greenest cities in the world, completely powered by renewable energy!

EXTREME RATING: 7/10

Underground town

Coober Pedy was once a tiny desert settlement in South Australia, with temperatures of up to 50°C in the summer. Not necessarily a place where many people would want to settle. But in 1915, a boy discovered an opal there, and suddenly Coober Pedy became an opal boom town!

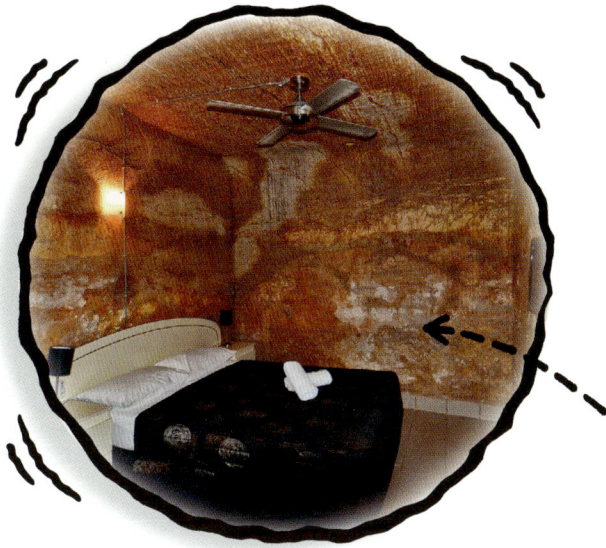

Coober Pedy opals

The heat in the town is so intense that many of the 2,500 residents live underground in hollowed-out caves.

An underground bedroom, Coober Pedy.

All under one roof

In Whittier, Alaska, winters are harsh, with 22 hours of darkness each day, and as much as 6 m of snow. So people shelter indoors, in a 14-storey building that's home to most of the town's residents!

Begich Towers has everything its inhabitants might need: a post office, grocery shop, medical clinic and church, while a school is connected by a tunnel to the block. You don't ever need to go outside!

I THINK I'LL STAY INDOORS THIS YEAR!

Begich Towers is home to about 300 people.

Can you build a city in 15 minutes?

Er – no. But a '15-minute city' **IS** in city designers' plans as they aim to make cities more sustainable places to live – along with other exciting new ideas.

I CAN'T EVEN GET OUT OF THE HOUSE IN 15 MINUTES!

 While 15-minute cities are still in the planning, here are some ways cities are already working towards a cleaner, more sustainable future:

Growing food locally reduces the distance food travels, cutting pollution and energy use. **Paris** is home to the world's biggest urban farm – built on rooftops!

 Nairobi, capital city of Kenya, is a leader in renewable energy with over 80 per cent of its energy coming from sustainable sources.

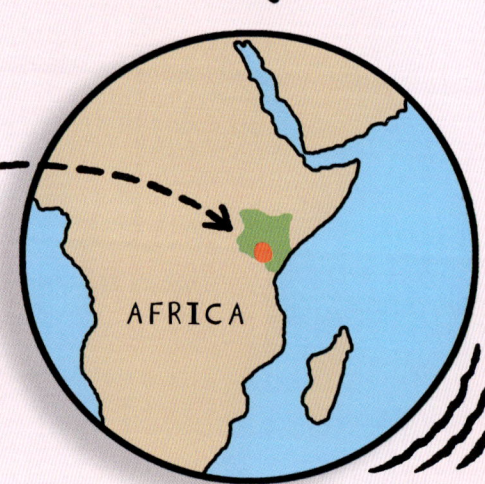

AFRICA

EUROPE

Reykjavik in Iceland is still ahead though, with ALL of its energy sourced from renewables.

In **Copenhagen** in Denmark, half of the population commutes to school or work by bike on the huge cycle superhighways that criss-cross the city.

➜ Fast town

In a 15-minute city, residents would be able to reach virtually everything they need, from schools and shops to parks and doctors' surgeries, within a 15-minute walk or bike ride. This way of living drastically cuts down on air pollution from cars, and means cities are greener, cleaner and more connected.

IT KEEPS ME FIT TOO!

There are already **16 cities** worldwide, including Paris and Shanghai, that have either implemented the 15-minute city idea or are working on it.

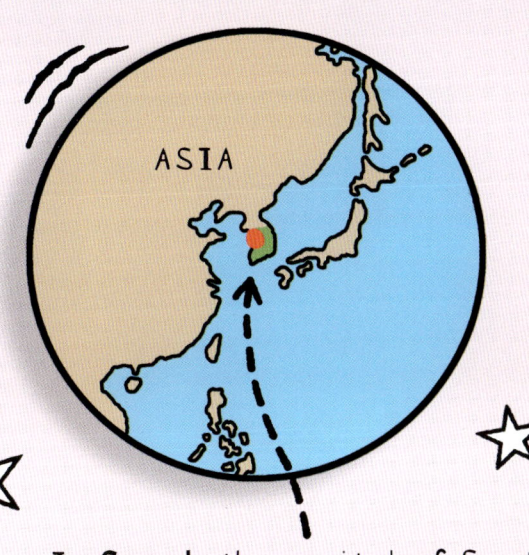

ASIA

Wellington in New Zealand has an eco-sanctuary in the city, where **40 rare native species** are protected, including the flightless takahe.

AUSTRALASIA

In **Seoul**, the capital of South Korea, waste food is collected and turned into fertiliser, animal food and fuel to heat homes.

SQUAWK!

San Francisco in the USA is known as the 'king of recycling' as **80 per cent** of its waste is sent to reuse and recycling schemes every year.

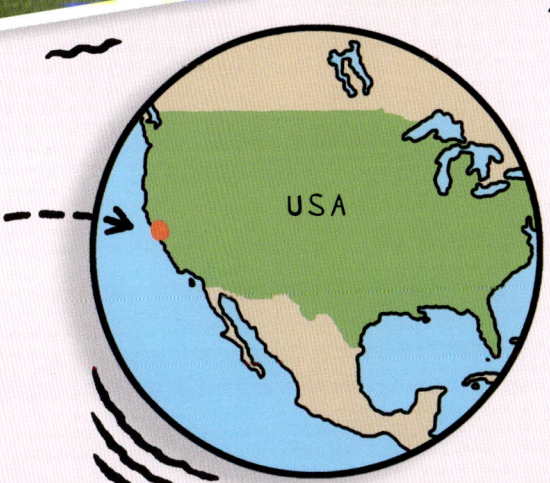

USA

Why are some people always on the move?

WE JUST CAN'T KEEP STILL!

Some people don't live in permanent settlements. Instead, they move around – often for work, but sometimes because of history or traditions.

Goats grazing by two gers in Mongolia.

Moving with the herd

Across the world, groups of people move around with their livestock, or animals. Around 30 per cent of the population of Mongolia are nomads, and live in communities that travel with their herds of cattle, goats and sheep in search of fresh grass for the animals to graze. Their homes are yurts or gers – large circular tents, traditionally made of wood, felt and animal skins.

Moving with the seasons

Many people travel for work. This can be seasonal, as people move away to work for a few weeks or months, often around harvest time when there is a sudden boom in farming jobs. They then return home, only to move back again for the next harvest!

Seasonal construction workers in Dubai, UAE.

Moving with the work

Other moves can be more permanent, for example when people move to work in a place for a few years for a particular reason, such as a big building project.

THIS IS DEFINITELY THE LIFE!

Digital nomads

The Internet and a handy laptop allows many people to work away from an office. This freedom has meant that some can choose to work anywhere in the world, so long as they have WiFi access! It offers the opportunity to travel the world and work from different locations.

Quick-fire questions

One, Central Park in Sydney, Australia, has 250 plant and flower species growing along its walls.

When is a building alive?

When it's a living building! Architects are designing city buildings to be as sustainable as possible. Living buildings feature green roofs and walls to absorb CO_2 and reduce air pollution, and provide shelter and food for city animals. Some new sustainable buildings even produce their own energy and harvest rainwater.

Which settlements go with the flow?

WE LIKE OUR SPACE!

Linear settlements! These settlements often grew up along the line of a transport route (line-ar, get it?), such as a road or river. They may originally have consisted of just a row of houses, strung out along either side of the route.

WE LIKE TO BE CLOSE TOGETHER!

By contrast, nucleated or cluster settlements develop around an important landmark or a building. Here, the buildings 'cluster' close together.

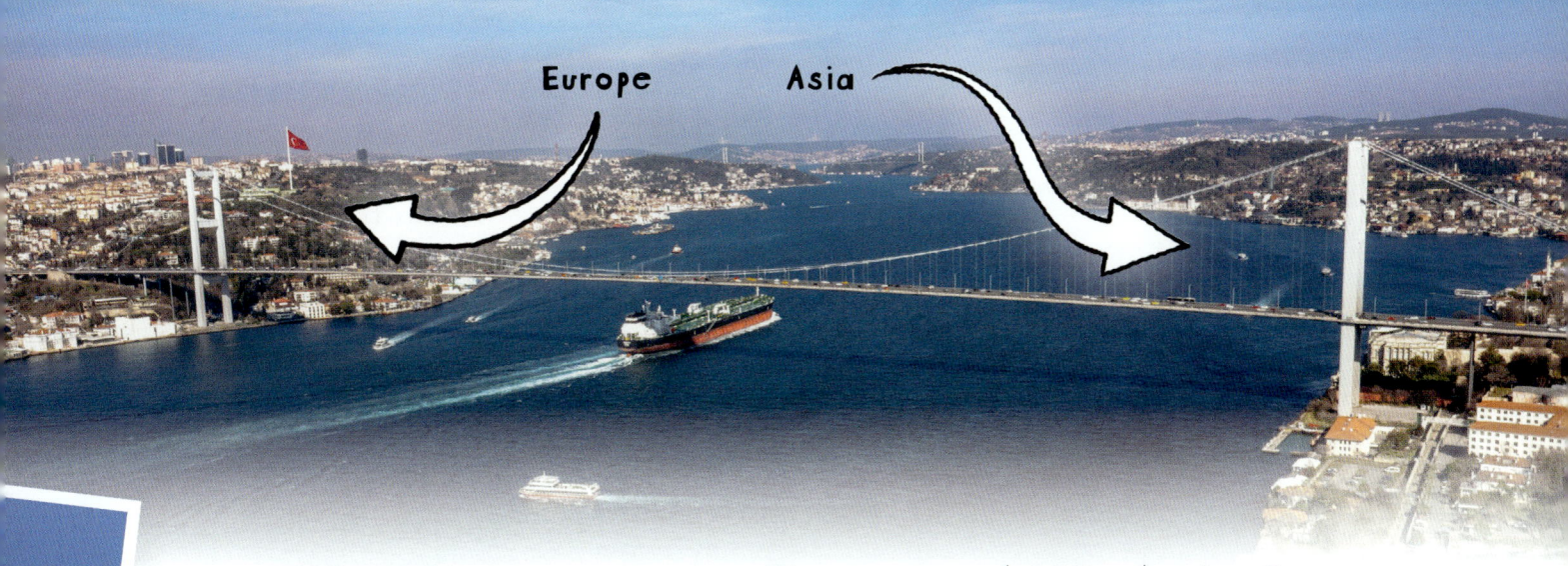

Europe

Asia

Which city is in Europe AND Asia?

ISTANBUL! This ancient city in Turkey has a unique location; it is the only city in the world to be on two continents at once – Europe and Asia. The Bosporus Strait, which links the Black Sea with the Mediterranean Sea, cuts the city in half. This makes the city an important trade route, and it has been a centre of political and religious history for more than 2,000 years.

Where is the most remote settlement in the world?

This award goes to Edinburgh of the Seven Seas, a tiny village on the volcanic island of Tristan da Cunha in the South Atlantic Ocean. Its 250 inhabitants live around 2,800 km off the coast of South Africa, and the island can only be reached by boat – a journey which takes almost a week!

WELCOME TO THE WORLD'S MOST REMOTE VILLAGE. YEP, YOU'RE REALLY FAR AWAY FROM ANYWHERE!

Glossary

Climate change The gradual change of weather patterns, caused by the warming of Earth's atmosphere due to increased CO2 emissions.

Colony An area or country that is controlled by another country.

Commute The journey people make between home and where they work.

Dormitory town An area where people live, and from where they travel to work in a nearby city every day.

Engineer A person who designs, builds or repairs machinery or structures, such as roads and bridges.

Indigenous People who are Indigenous belong to a community that originally inhabited an area, before settlers from other countries arrived.

Industrial Revolution A period of time when many new machines were invented. They were used in factories to produce more goods much faster. The Industrial Revolution began in Britain in around 1760 and spread around the world.

Irrigate To deliver water to plants and crops, often by building waterways.

Natural resources Substances or materials that are found in nature, such as sunlight, wood and water.

Nomad A person who doesn't live in the same place all year round. A digital nomad is someone who moves around and works online from wherever they are.

Opal A valuable gemstone, often used in jewellery.

Parliament The people who have been elected to make laws for a region or country.

Public services Services that are available to all members of a community, such as waste collection, healthcare, libraries and education.

Reclaim To start using something again that had been lost or forgotten.

Reservoir A large artificial lake, used to store and supply water.

Rural Describing something related to the countryside.

Suburb A settlement on the outskirts of a city.

Sustainable Designed to use as few natural resources as possible over a long period of time. Because of this, sustainable products are more environmentally friendly.

Urban Describing something related to cities.

Further reading

Websites

www.bbc.co.uk/teach/class-clips-video/geography-ks1 --ks2-cities-towns-villages/zjn492p

This short film looks at the key features of villages, towns and cities.

www.youtube.com/watch?v=naPguX84Amg

Watch this video to find out more about Whittier, Alaska, from someone who lives there.

www.youtube.com/watch?v=8n9PbHXA6Lo

What it's like to live underground in Coober Pedy, and where the town gets its energy from.

Books

World Feature Focus – Settlements
by Rebecca Kahn (Franklin Watts, 2021)

If the World Were 100 People
by Jackie McCann and Aaron Cushley (Harper Collins, 2021)

A City Through Time
by Steve Noon, Matilda Gollon and Sheila Collins (DK, 2021)

Index